Tips for Effective Management

By Andrew Vanderdussen

May 2019

Table of Contents

Executives are masters at delegation, so copy them

Avoid the untouchables

Be careful with friendships

Perfect your horse trading skills

Final thoughts

Also by this Author on Amazon

World War II: A Narrative History

Stupid Leaders

Stupid Sports

Stupid Bosses

Introduction

Good managers are hard to find. Restricted budgets, lazy employees, and union regulations are just some of the obstacles facing them. This assumes the manager is trying their best. Some organizations view management positions as a sinecure, a reward for decades of service and a soft glide path towards retirement.

Naturally employees saddled with do nothing managers resent the situation they are faced with. But there are many managers who try their best and still fail. This list is for them, a roadmap of sorts to detect and avoid the landmines waiting for them.

Before You Accept a Management Position

Many employees accept a promotion to manager without thinking twice. But be careful! Danger may be lurking.

Consider the circumstances

If the promotion seems to be too good to be true, back off and examine the situation. Why did the previous manager leave? For example, Steve made the jump from small 750 employee organization to a manager position in a Fortune 500 company. Everything seemed great until he found a disgruntled employee who thought he deserved the post instead. Previous managers had come and gone, unable to address or resolve the problem. Knowing the toxic situation, internal candidates passed on the offer. But Steve didn't know all this. He came in unawares from outside the organization and was ambushed. While he was able to get the problem employee transferred, it took all of his political capital to do so and crippled his relationship with the rest of the team. More detailed questions during the interview process could have helped Steve.

Ask plenty of questions during the interview process

If you don't define the scope and responsibilities of the team up front, they will be defined by someone else. Make sure you fully understand expectations and requirements. What performance numbers will you have to meet? Ask if the previous manager met those numbers to determine whether immediate improvements will be needed.

If you don't know your executive, they won't know you either.

Executive support is critical to any management position. This is the person responsible for approving resources, headcount, budget, and everything else necessary for the team to operate. If you don't control these items yourself, find out who does and cultivate good relations with them. You may need support from more than one executive, so cast your net wide when searching for support.

Make sure your team's value to the business is defined up front.

If your team is viewed as overhead you are doomed from the start. Find out the team's value to the business, and make it your first priority to enhance and build that perception.

Be aware of Union Requirements and other labor issues

If your team is global, employees in different regions will have to be handled according to local regulations. Additional resources may be needed, and you must have those resources up front before taking over the team. If you are unsure, get agreements in writing from the executives.

Leadership Training Matters

Many employees expect to inherit management positions through seniority. However their previous skillset may not prepare them for leadership. Caught unawares, employees without leadership training are fighting with one or both hands tied behind their backs.

If you haven't had leadership training already, arrange for it as part of the interview process. Many Fortune 500 companies offer it as part of their training regimen. If you are with a smaller organization, seek outside training and have the company pay for it.

Beware of the Bait and Switch

If a team is going downhill, don't go with them. Organizations may be scheduled for elimination and outsourcing to overseas entities. You do not want to be the last manager of a dying team. Be aware of the strategic situation before accepting an offer, particularly if no one else wants it.

Be sensitive to employee feelings

Use the interview process to measure your new team's mental mindset. Some employees may have expected the position that you are taking. Be sensitive to their feelings and make sure they understand their importance to the team and the organization.

Determine the Area that needs your Attention

When you take over a team you cannot focus on everything. Identify the critical areas that need to be addressed first. Don't give the operations folks all the attention and leave the developers hanging. Particularly if development is a problem area that needs fixing. Executives and employees already know the problem areas and will lose confidence in your management abilities if you make the wrong choice. First impressions matter in dating and in management.

You're Really a Lawyer, Not a Manager

Make your case

Have you seen lawyers make their case in court? Managers have to present arguments on a daily basis. Your judge is the executive and the jury consists of other teams in the organization that need to be convinced. Whether asking for more resources, presenting project plans for approval, or addressing employee complaints with Human Resources, you will need to make your case over and over again.

Present your evidence

Without evidence lawyers are crippled, and so are you. Much of your time will be spent gathering data. Whether researching the right technology, gathering competitive price quotes, or estimating resource hours needed for project completion, you will need data at your fingertips. Convert your employees into evidence gathering teams.

If you don't believe it, no one else will

Sometimes evidence is not enough. You have to convince the jury. Sway the public. Persuade your executive. But you can't do any of those things if you don't believe in the case that you are presenting. That means bring passion, commitment, and a sense of certainty to every argument you make. Others will sense a lack of confidence and torpedo your project plans.

Know the law better than anyone else

Company policies and procedures are to you what the law is to the courts. Familiarize yourself with them and understand which ones have teeth. Some policies are enforced while others are just there for show. Knowing the difference can mean the winning or losing against other managers and organizations.

Adjust to the unexpected

Surprises don't just happen in court. Economic fluctuations can lead to sudden budget cuts. Successful organizations can spring new acquisition and integration projects without warning. Employees can leave without notice. Whatever happens, as manager you will need to react rapidly to unexpected problems.

Never Accept Additional Workload Quietly

If you absorb additional work the executives will just pile on more

Absorbing work is a one way street. Once you take it on you can never give it back. Executives love to offload tasks. Organizations tend to overload their teams, particularly the ones that are labeled as overhead. That's why it's critical to show the impact of any additional work laid on the team.

Show the impact

When you receive additional workload, show the impact to your team. Document how other projects were pushed back to accommodate the new project. Show the increased load of incident tickets and lengthened time to resolution statistics.

Practice your "mamma mia" routine

Sometimes logical discussion is not enough. In certain organizations you have to stand on the table and shout before anyone notices. But any noise you make should be calculated. Remain under control and create a performance that will get your critical situation noticed without offending others. Be prepared to use that routine more than once as crises tend to come in bunches.

Be Aware of the Total Project and Resource Burden

If your team cannot absorb the additional work, someone else must be available to take it on. Collect intelligence on other team's project and resource loads. Use this information to propose alternate teams to absorb the additional load, particularly for busy work that would detract from your critical business tasks.

Demand additional resources along with the extra work

Teams tend to remain static over time. Headcount will only be added with appropriate justification. Extra work is often the only justification that will be accepted. Don't pass up the opportunity to ask for more resources. Being a good soldier and not asking for help will only aid your competitors who have already requested more resources.

Be Prepared to Compete with Other Teams

Resources are Limited

Executives must choose which teams get the resources. Your team will compete with other organizations for support and attention. Any resources you do not secure will go to someone else.

Gather intelligence on other teams

You cannot win a contest without knowing what your opponents have. Make sure to gather Intel on your competitors. Know their project list and resources available. Understand the strengths and weaknesses of their employees. Structure your team strengths and resource justifications to that data. While you may enjoy friendly relationships with other teams, never forget that you are competing with them. What is best for the organization can work to your advantage.

Avoid the dumping ground

While teams work to acquire resources, they are also racing to dump unwanted busy work on other organizations. Don't be the good soldier manager that completes all the grinding tasks while other groups seize all the glory projects. It's like a game of musical chairs. Last manager standing is stuck with all of the leftover scraps.

Don't miss the boat

Many managers are discouraged by lack of resources and the grind of running the office. In their frustration they sit on their hands and let opportunities slip by. Remember that taking on exciting projects is one of the few justifications you will have for adding headcount and resources. When opportunities come, stand up and be counted. Seize the moment and be the first to propose a plan to address the business needs.

Expand the knowledge base

Experienced managers can be complacent. After years of duty they think they've seen it all. That is rarely the case. More often managers who think they are secure in their positions are passed up by younger, hungrier people who are eager to learn. Stay on top of current trends and adjust your team's focus to address them.

Executive Love Visual Graphs

Seeing is believing

Executives get bored with statistics. Colorful graphs and flashy headers are more their style. Long pages of unending text will bore them to sleep. Make your presentation is visual and interesting to keep their attention.

Tailor to their interests

Find out your executive's priorities and shape your presentation to them. If you don't give them what they want, someone else will.

One page summaries are popular

Executives are under time pressure. They do not have hours to sit and listen. Make sure all of your key points are on the first summary page. If the executive is called away on urgent business, you already have your ideas planted in their minds.

If You are not the Most Important Manager, Someone Else will be

Managers are ranked too

When you rank your employees from best to worst, remember that executives do the same thing with managers. You will be rated in comparison to your peers. Understand the competition. Know where you stand in the pecking order. Study your peer managers and categorize their strengths and weaknesses. Use that information to your advantage.

Good soldiers finish last

Running the office may keep your team employed, but it will not attract any attention. Seize the opportunity for new and exciting projects. Shoulder your way to the head of the line. Make the executives understand why you and your team are critical to the business.

Repetition is the key

Don't rest on your laurels. Some managers complete a big project and ride that one wave to the end. Executives are a "what have you done for me lately" crowd. Remind them regularly of your team's value and accomplishments. Several medium successful projects will often outshine one big project. Repeated success will stick in their heads, while one big project will be forgotten over time.

Government agencies are also competitive

Public sector managers sometimes think they have it made. Regularly scheduled annual increases are like gold. Until the government cuts back. High performing managers will be protected while low performing ones will be frozen out or starved to death. Instead of fighting for private sector profits, you are competing with other government agencies. Public sector competition can be just as nasty and cutthroat as in the private sector.

Don't Neglect Training for your Employees

Make room in the budget

Budgets are always under pressure and training is usually the first target. Don't succumb to temptation. Employees need training to achieve and retain expert levels of competence. Without refreshers their expertise levels will gradually erode over time.

Customize training for each employee

One size does not fit all. Make sure the training for each employee matches their interests and skill set requirements for the position. Improvement must be measurable, otherwise you are wasting money and time.

Avoid the extra vacation time trap

Some employees view training as more paid vacation time. Particularly if the training is in Las Vegas or Florida. Avoid flashy venues and make sure employees are focused on the goal during training trips. Set measurable milestones to record progress and lessons learned. Have each employee do a presentation upon their return from training so that the entire team can see the benefits and improvements gained from the course.

Understand the employee mindset

Employees can be just like executives. What have you done for me lately? Managers are counted on for salary increases and training. Don't present the training as an obligation. Structure the training so it adds value to the employee's career. When the training is completed publicize the results and resulting employee successes.

Holding Grudges Harms You and Them

There's always another project

If a project goes badly, don't linger on it. Fix what you can and move on to the next project. Focus on a future success rather than past failure.

Ignore lingering employee complaints

As a manager you will be deluged with information. In many ways it's like babysitting. Some employee concerns are legitimate while others are not. Don't get caught up while employees with decades of service rant about how someone did them wrong. Cut through the whining and get to the core issue. Either resolve it or move on.

Build up good will with other managers

Some employees just don't fit. Personalities and attitudes matter. Remember that if they will not perform for you they may shine for someone else. Maintain good relationships with other managers. The day may come when you need to transfer a problem employee to them. It's a two way street, so you may accept employees also. Hoard your political capital for situations where you really need a favor.

If you're stuck with problem employees, move them out of harm's way

Some employees will continue to rant regardless of how you address their issues. You may not have the ability to transfer them elsewhere or get rid of them. If you are stuck with them, put them in areas to minimize the damage to the rest of the team. Keep them away from critical projects. Minimize or eliminate their exposure to the executives, as their behavior may reflect badly on you and your team.

Document and record

Verbal conversations are easily forgotten. Write down, document, and date critical conversations.

Executives can ask piercing questions and may not accept glib answers. Have documented records available to justify your actions and positions. If you are approached by HR or Legal, follow their instructions to the letter of the law or policy.

Keep it Professional

Some of the most intelligent people resort to name calling when they are frustrated. Calling people idiots or morons may please your ego but will lower your reputation with your peers. Name calling also shows a loss of control, which will cause your team to lose confidence in your ability to keep it together.

Have landing spots available

The time may come when you need to move on. Have landing spots available ahead of time. Strategize your career for your next promotion. Have a road map in your mind. If you cannot move up, seek out lateral teams you can move over to within the organization. Be aware of who else is retiring or moving on and research the possible openings.

Leaving the organization is a one way ticket

In larger organizations there are dozens of staff waiting for promotions. Manager and Director Positions are snapped up immediately when someone leaves. Don't think you can leave and come back. If you are making a lateral move, fine. But once you leave the organization it is almost impossible to return at the same level.

Have Patience

Rome wasn't built in a day

Take your time to build comprehensive project plans. Rushing into jury rigged solutions will only cause more pain in the long run.

Employees need time to develop

Mentors tend to get excited about their protégés. But you can't hurry them along. Let them absorb and perfect a few skills before pushing them into the next project or role.

Too Much information can overload your Executive

Measure your meetings with stakeholders. Since their time is limited, only bring up the most important items. Do not rush through status updates so fast that they cannot keep up with you.

Never let them see you sweat

Good managers swallow their complaints until off time after work. If you need to blow off steam, do it somewhere else. Employees, peers, and executives should never see you lose control.

Know your Place

Have the sense to stay in a good situation

We all have our comfort levels. While most people will automatically accept a promotion, think twice before leaving a good team. Are you moving up or moving down? Successful people do not take every offer, weighing the pros and cons before making a move. If the move does not help your career, you may be smarter to stay in place for less money.

Consider what came before you

Rich was a successful engineer. After seeing two managers come and go he was offered a promotion to manager. However Rich was aware that his predecessors, both good people he admired and respected, had been forced out for different reasons. Understanding the benefits did not outweigh the risks, Rich made the right decision to turn down the promotion and retain his engineering slot.

Don't make a rapid decision out of frustration

Many people are frustrated in their jobs. But consider that all moves are not up the ladder. In your haste you may be exchanging one disaster for another. Take a step back and analyze the situation logically and from several angles before making an emotional decision.

Don't accept a promotion you are not ready for

You can grow into some positions with the right sponsorship and support. Others are more demanding and require expertise right from the start. Make sure you have the tools on hand before moving into a challenging role.

Environments are not transferable

Success at a Fortune 500 organization may not translate to a smaller company. If you are fond of expensive tools and software, stay in larger organizations that have budget and resources. Smaller companies do not and will not have budget or staff to implement expensive or labor intensive solutions. If you want a retirement post with lowered requirements, fine. Just lower your expectations as well.

Moving around will not fix core issues

If you can't manage one team, there is no guarantee you can lead any other team. Take a hard look at your skills and address any deficiencies before transferring. Take feedback as constructive criticism and use it accordingly.

Hire Employees that are Smarter than You

Collect Talent

Don't be intimidated by highly skilled employees. Add them to your team before someone else grabs them. It's a zero sum game so you may need to offer incentives for an employee to work for you instead of another team.

Many employees are not interested in management

Management is one skill set among many. Employees with specialized skills know their roles and have no interest in leadership positions. Give these folks a home on your team where they can flourish.

Leverage smart employees to attract more of them

Word travels fast. Once your smart employees spread the news about your team, other qualified candidates will line up trying to get in. Create a snowball effect where your team is the destination of choice from both inside and outside the organization.

Play it Both Ways

Wear more than one hat

Different circumstances call for more than one role. Be the champion for improved performance and results. When the team is under pressure, switch roles and be the cheerleader who offers support. Make sure employees know that you are on their side.

Don't wear out the same message over and over

Repetition is useful, but don't overdo it. Employees quickly tire of the same vision statement repeated again and again. Mix things up. Plan getaways and fun activities to break up the monotony of running the shop.

Communication with stakeholders is different than communication with employees

It is not enough to change the content of your presentation for different audiences. Make changes to your demeanor as well. Employees may desire a more informal approach while executives could require a more formal appearance and delivery. Enthusiasm can mean more than facts and figures. If the audience does not believe in you, they will not accept your content, regardless of how well researched or factual it may be.

Executives are Masters of Delegation, so copy them

Executives know how to Delegate

Successful executives delegate tasks to trusted team members. Their time is precious and so is yours. Micromanagement can burn out the most talented managers. Delegate tasks to lighten the load.

Find out which employees you can trust

Trust is a prerequisite for delegation of tasks. Find out which employees can handle critical tasks. Prioritize tasks and assign the busy work to less capable staff.

Once you delegate, stop worrying

Don't second guess yourself. Once you delegate a task give your employees space to complete it. There will be time enough to check on progress in the status update meetings. Worrying about status all the time is a waste of energy.

Avoid the Untouchables

Go around obstacles

Some executives, directors, and managers received their positions as a sinecure. A reward for previous performance. Or it might be nepotism. Whatever the reason is, their positions are secure regardless of performance. When some managers find this out, they get angry or make a scene. This will only anger the secure person's sponsor. Don't make enemies by pointing out a situation that you cannot change. Accept the reality of the situation and work around it.

Don't waste time pointing out the obvious

There are few secrets in organizations. If someone is underperforming everyone already knows. Don't act like Sherlock Holmes and lecture people about the obvious. Your sense of righteousness may rub others the wrong way and create enemies that you do not need.

Time is on your side

No matter how secure a person is, things change over time. CEOs leave and organizational protection vanishes. Sometimes the underperformer sees the writing on the wall and quietly retires. Wait for the moment of vulnerability before you move in to attack. Open your mouth too early and an opportunity could be spoiled before the time is right.

Encourage underperformers to leave

Sometimes the obstacles are on your own team. Despite your best efforts, some employees may never get their act straight. Don't waste time arguing with your executive if the employee cannot be let go. Instead, take an indirect approach by assigning them annoying busy work. Eliminate/reduce training for them and limit the resources available for their minor projects. Without being obvious, let them know it's time to move on.

Be Careful with Friendships

University colleagues may not make good employees

Contacts formed over years of education can be useful. But they are not automatic. Don't let your friendship blind you to weaknesses or deficiencies. Hiring a friend can turn into a disaster and ruin years of warm relations. Do your homework and evaluate a friend objectively, like any other candidate.

Things change over time

A colleague from years ago may share a history of successful projects completed. But yesterday's success may not translate into better work today. If your friend has not kept their skills up to date they may stumble on challenging projects. Be aware of any changes at work or home that my affect your colleagues performance.

Paths can diverge when goals change

Your career path may be different from a friend's trajectory. If your colleague is satisfied with their position, you may be hungry for other challenges. Don't drag them to a place they don't want to go based on friendship. Sometimes the best move is to leave a friend behind and forge ahead in a new direction.

Expand your circle

Some managers establish a team of trusted colleagues and carry that group with them for decades. While this may give you a comfort level, creating a clique may limit your opportunities to meet new friends and expand the team's base of expertise. Time and attrition can erode the circle of colleagues, so replenish the pool with new talent additions.

Perfect Your Horse Trading Skills

More time is spent negotiating than building

Building systems and environments is not difficult. The problem is fighting through restricted budgets and complex design sessions to get there. Since you will never have enough budget for everything, your first budget proposal should contain placeholders. These items are not critical and are there for horse trading purposes. When the inevitable cutbacks occur you will have items ready to be eliminated while your critical projects are fully funded.

Create dependencies

Construct environments with business value for multiple departments. This will create automatic alliances with other managers who need your system to operate. When the bean counters and auditors come you will have a network of business stakeholders to speak in your defense.

Give the auditors small wins

Auditors need to show progress and accomplishment. Give them small wins in non-critical areas that make their reports look good. In exchange they will understand that the business comes first and let the revenue generating systems operate.

Make vendors compete for you

Sometimes vendors get lazy and expect regularly scheduled orders to continue. Don't let them get complacent. Push them for discounts and pressure them by mentioning the competitive environment. Only offer long term contracts for deep discounts and incentives.

Final Thoughts

Having suffered through 300 page documents, I have tried to make this concise and relevant. If you enjoyed the book, please take the time to give it a good review!

www.ingramcontent.com/pod-product-compliance
Lightning Source LLC
Chambersburg PA
CBHW030738180526
45157CB00008BA/3224